Matt?

by Tamera Williams
illustrated by Mike Reid

Practice Decodable 7

McGraw Hill Education

Bothell, WA • Chicago, IL • Columbus, OH • New York, NY

MHEonline.com

Send all inquiries to:
McGraw-Hill Education
8787 Orion Place
Columbus, OH 43240

ISBN: 978-0-02-145979-7
MHID: 0-02-145979-7

Printed in China

8 9 10 11 12 DSS 27 26 25 24 23

I am Tam.

Matt?

I am Sam.

Matt?

I am Matt.

Tam, Sam, and Matt.